The Riot Group

PUGILIST SPECIALIST

by **Adriano Shaplin**

Pugilist Specialist was originally produced by The Riot Group and Chantal Arts + Theatre. It opened at the Pleasance Theatre, Edinburgh on 1 August 2003 as part of the Edinburgh Festival Fringe. The original cast were:

Lt. Emma Stein	Stephanie Viola
Lt. Studdard	Drew Friedman
Lt. Travis Freud	Adriano Shaplin
Col. Johns	Paul Schnabel
Directed and designed by	The Riot Group
Original Sound	Adriano Shaplin
Stage Manager	Maria Shaplin

The production transferred to the Soho Theatre + Writers' Centre on 14 January 2004, followed by a tour of the UK and Eire. *Pugilist Specialist* will open at the new 59E59 Theatre in New York from 14 September 2004.

This production won *The Scotsman's* First of the Firsts Award, *The Scotsman's* Fringe First Award and *The Herald* Angel Award and was nominated for *The Stage's* Best Ensemble Acting Award 2003.

PUGILIST SPECIALIST
by **Adriano Shaplin**

Lt. Emma Stein	**Stephanie Viola**
Lt. Studdard	**Drew Friedman**
Lt. Travis Freud	**Adriano Shaplin**
Col. Johns	**Paul Schnabel**

directed and designed by	**The Riot Group**
stage manager	**Maria Shaplin**
production manager and lighting designer	**Adrian Bristow**
original sound designer	**Adriano Shaplin**
graphic designer	**Huw Jenkins**
	M + H Communications Ltd
photography	**Robbie Jack**
press contact:	**Louise Chantal**
	(020 7439 1175, www.chantalarts.co.uk)

The company would like to thank:
Adrian Bristow and Shakti from The Garage Theatre; Pleasance Theatre Festival Ltd and Christopher Richardson; The Fringe Society; Mark Brown; Jon Fawcett and the Riverside Studios; Everyone at Soho Theatre Company; the Institute of Ideas; James Caygill and SDA Print Ltd; Nick Salmon, Alexis Meech and the Theatre Investment Fund; Lee Menzies and all at the TIF offices; and Josie Shaeffer.

The Riot Group

Since 1997, The Riot Group has brought uncompromised intensity to the world of contemporary theatre. Tightly-knit and fiercely committed, this small ensemble has produced a string of original performance pieces which combine absurd comedy and powerful political satire with a confrontational acting style.

In the past seven years, The Riot Group has produced six original plays and has toured to festivals and theatres throughout the US and Europe, winning recognition for outstanding new writing and ensemble acting. *Wreck the Airline Barrier (1999)*, *Victory at the Dirt Palace (2002)*, and *Pugilist Specialist (2003)*, were all awarded the coveted Edinburgh Fringe First award and Herald Angel award, while *Pugilist Specialist* was also the winner of *The Scotsman*'s 2003 First of the Fringe Firsts award.

All Riot Group performance texts are written by Adriano Shaplin with roles tailored to each individual actor. Each production is collaboratively directed and designed by the cast. The Riot Group is currently composed of five company members: Adriano Shaplin (writer/artistic director), Stephanie Viola, Drew Friedman, Paul Schnabel, and Maria Shaplin.

The Riot Group is dedicated to maintaining an ongoing ensemble while fostering relationships with like-minded organizations and artists.

www.theriotgroup.com

Chantal Arts + Theatre Ltd

CAT is a company set up in 2003 by Louise Chantal, whose previous production and marketing experience includes the Soho Theatre + Writers' Centre, Pleasance Theatres and Actors Touring Company. CAT specializes in working with new writing and international companies. Recent or current productions include: The Riot Group's *Victory at the Dirt Palace* (London season and national tour 2003); *Roadmovie* by Nick Whitfield and Wes Williams (Edinburgh Festival 2002 and UK and Eire tour 2003); *Silent Engine* by Julian Garner (with Pentabus Theatre – Fringe First winner Edinburgh Festival 2002 and UK Tour) and a British Council tour in Israel of *The Government Inspector* by Theatre de l'Ange Fou.

Recent and current marketing and press clients include: Bryony Lavery's *Precious Bane* for Pentabus Theatre; Birmingham Stage Company's *Collision* by Dominic Leyton at the Old Red Lion; Suspect Package Theatre Company in *Problem Child* by George F Walker at the New End; Brand X in DIE at the Riverside Studios; and the Caird Company and Theatre of Angels *Theatre Café* at the Arcola Theatre in April/May 2003.

The company undertakes a variety of roles including producing and general management, tour booking, marketing and PR. Please call Louise Chantal on 020 7436 1175 for further information.

www.chantalarts.co.uk

3rd Floor, 118 Wardour Street
London W1V 3LA
email: louisejchantal@aol.com
tele: 020 7439 1175 fax: 020 7434 0932

The Theatre Investment Fund
Pugilist Specialist was produced with the assistance of a New Producer's Bursary from the Theatre Investment Fund, which is a registered charity (no. 271349). The TIF assists new producers and invests in productions throughout the UK. The producer would like to extend her thanks to the following supporters of the Theatre Investment Fund:

The Society of London Theatre
The Arts Council of England
The Mackintosh Foundation
Clear Channel Entertainment UK
The Equity Trust Fund

PUGILIST SPECIALIST TOUR 2004

Tour details correct at time of going to press.
Further information: www.chantalarts.co.uk / 020 7439 1175

Soho Theatre + Writers' Centre 21 Dean St, London W1	Weds 14 Jan – Sat 7 Feb at 7.30pm (matinees 24, 31 Jan & 7 Feb at 4pm)
Old Museum Theatre, Belfast	Weds 11 Jan – Sat 14 Feb
The Helix, Dublin	Tues 17 Feb – Sat 21 Feb
The Arches, Glasgow	Tues 24 Feb – Sat 28 Feb
Oxford Playhouse	Mon 1 March
The Gulbenkian, Canterbury	Weds 3 March
The Drama Centre, Cambridge	Thurs 4 March
The Nuffield, Southampton	Fri 5 – Sat 6 March
Bonnington Theatre, Notts	Tues 9 March
Sherman Theatre, Cardiff	Weds 10 March
Unity Theatre, Liverpool	Fri 12 – Sat 13 March
The Drum, Theatre Royal, Plymouth	Mon 15 – Sat 20 March
Leeds Metropolitan University	Tues 23 – Weds 24 March
Theatre in the Mill, Bradford	Thurs 25 March
Selby Arts Centre	Fri 26 March
Contact Theatre, Manchester	Mon 29 March – Saturday 3 April
KOMEDIA, Brighton (as part of the Brighton International Festival)	Tues 11 – Sat 15 May
The Door, Birmingham Rep	Tues 18 – Sat 22 May
Swindon Arts Centre	Tues 25 May
The Hawth, Crawley	Thurs 27 May
Trinity Arts Centre, Tunbridge Wells	Fri 28 May
New Greenham Arts, Newbury	Sat 29 May

Pugilist Specialist will open at the 59E59 St Theatre in New York from 14 September 2004.
www.59e59.org

● soho
● theatre company

Soho is passionate in its commitment to new writing, producing a year-round programme of bold, original and accessible new plays – many of them from first-time playwrights.

'a foundry for new talent...one of the country's leading producer's of new writing' Evening Standard

Soho aims to be the first port of call for the emerging writer and combines the process of production with the process of development. The unique Writers' Centre invites writers at any stage of their career to submit scripts and receives, reads and reports on over 2,000 per year. In addition to the national Verity Bargate Award – a competition aimed at new writers – it runs an extensive series of programmes to develop writers not just in the theatre but also for radio, TV and film.

'a creative hotbed...not only the making of theatre but the cradle for new screenplay and television scripts' The Times

Contemporary, comfortable, air-conditioned and accessible, the Soho Theatre is busy from early morning to late at night. Alongside the production of new plays, it's also an intimate venue to see leading international comedians.

'there's a staggering amount of first class comedy to be found in Dean Street' The Daily Telegraph

● soho
● friends

People say you can't put a price on friendship. They're wrong.

Soho Theatre Company has launched a new Friends scheme to support its work in developing new writers and reaching new audiences. To find out how to become a Soho Friend and what we will give you in return, contact the development department on 020 7478 0111, email development@sohotheatre.com or visit www.sohotheatre.com.

Please help us to continue and expand our work. Please become a friend.

● soho
● theatre + writers' centre

Soho Theatre + Writers' Centre
21 Dean Street, London W1D 3NE
Admin: 020 7287 5060
Fax: 020 7287 5061
Box Office: 020 7478 0100 Minicom: 020 7478 0136

Bars and Restaurant
Café Lazeez brasserie serves Indian-fusion dishes until 12pm. Late bar open until 1am. The Terrace Bar serves a range of soft and alcoholic drinks.

Email information list
For regular programme updates and offers, subscribe to our free email bulletins: www.sohotheatre.com/mailing

If you would like to make any comments about any of the productions seen at Soho Theatre, why not visit our chatroom at www.sohotheatre.com

Artistic Director: Abigail Morris
Assistant to Artistic Director: Nadine Hoare
Administrative Producer: Mark Godfrey
Assistant to Administrative Producer: Tim Whitehead
Writers' Centre Director: Nina Steiger
Associate Director: Jonathan Lloyd
Casting Director: Ginny Schiller
Marketing and Development Director: Zoe Reed
Development Officer: Gayle Rogers
Marketing Consultant: Jacqui Gellman
Marketing and Development Assistant: Kelly Duffy
Press Officer: Nancy Poole
General Manager: Catherine Thornborrow
Front of House and Building Manager: Anne Mosley
Financial Controller: Kevin Dunn
Book Keeper: Elva Tehan
Box Office and IT Manager: Kate Truefitt
Deputy Box Office Manager: Steve Lock
Box Office Assistant: Janice Draper, Jennie Fellows, Richard Gay, Leah Read, Will Sherriff-Hammond, Natalie Worrall and Kalai Yung
Duty Managers: Morag Brownlie, Mike Owen and Rebecca Storey
Front of House Staff: Louise Beere, Helene Le Bohec, Sharon Degan, Matthew Halpin, Sioban Hyams, Grethe Jensenl, Sam Laydon, Katherine Smith, Harriet Spencer, Rebecca Storey, Luke Tebbutt, Katherine Smith, Rachel Southern, Rachel Bavidge, Neli Maclennan, Carole Menduni and Jamie Zubairi
Production Manager: Nick Ferguson
Chief Technician: Nick Blount
Chief LX: Christoph Wagner
Lighting Technician: Ade Peterkin

PUGILIST SPECIALIST

First published in this version in 2003 by Oberon Books Ltd.
(incorporating Absolute Classics)
521 Caledonian Road, London N7 9RH
Tel: 020 7607 3637 / Fax: 020 7607 3629

e-mail: oberon.books@btinternet.com
www.oberonbooks.com

A catalogue record for this book is available from the
British Library.

ISBN: 1 84002 410 0

Cover design by Huw Jenkins for M+H Communications
Photograph by Robbie Jack

Printed in Great Britain by Antony Rowe Ltd, Chippenham.

Characters

LT. EMMA STEIN

LT. STUDDARD

LT. TRAVIS FREUD

COL. JOHNS

Notes on the Play

This play was written for the Riot Group. The roles were designed for members of the ensemble, to be performed in accordance with a developing company aesthetic. This text represents neither the raw material for, nor a faithful transcript of, those performances. The text is just one unfixed, unfinished component of a dialogue between author and ensemble, performance and audience.

The locations suggested by the action are a barracks, an airplane, a desert.

Notes on Production

On stage there are two wooden benches, each approximately twelve feet long. They are composed of a flat surface and two legs. No backing. Hanging from the ceiling directly above the benches is a plain microphone.

With the exception of scenes toward the end, the action is expressed as audio, suggesting a transcript or taped conversation. No naturalistic movement accompanies the entrances, exits, or travel. Actors face forward on the front two benches when they are in a scene. There is a measure of gestured movement including head turns, nods, and hand movement. Imagine actors in a studio recording a live radio play. Transitions and reconfigurations of bodies or benches will occur during light changes.

On stage there are two wooden benches, each approximately twelve feet long. They are composed of a flat surface and two legs. No backing. Hanging from the ceiling directly above the benches is a plain microphone.

With the exception of scenes toward the end, the action is expressed as audio, suggesting a transcript or taped conversation. No naturalistic movement accompanies the entrances, exits, or travel. Actors face forward. There is a measure of gestured movement including head turns, nods, and hand movement. Imagine actors in a studio recording a live radio play. Transitions and reconfigurations of bodies or benches will occur during light changes. These transitions indicate a shift in tone, time, or place.

LT. STEIN: Loneliness. Mother of grief. I'm early. I am an unwilling preface. That's me. They make promises. Clean breaks. Smash and grab. Quick in-and-out. I know they expect an audience, otherwise my sex would exclude me. They never invite the girls in uniform and forget the cameras. I polish my teeth more often than my boots, unfortunately. I've been instructed to embrace my role as military spokes model. Never mind my expertise, that is more judiciously employed. Meaning rarely. But here I am. Early. This prevents the boys from rehearsing limericks or carving their fantastic gynecological reliefs in the tabletops. Male gossip stinks like napalm in a room, arrive last and you'll see how it makes your eyes water. Punctuality is my feminism. (*Checks watch.*) Five minutes to go.

Pause.

What's your story? Were you an athlete in school? A lesbian? Was your poor redneck father buried with his boots on? That's okay. Let the boys think whatever. I believe in origins. There are worse things than stories. Worse indignities than explanation. Secrets are my armor. Silence is my camouflage. Victory forgives dishonesty. We won't call it a preface. We'll call it a prayer. Loneliness, grief, discipline. Spectacles, testicles, wallet, watch. Decode that.

Transition.

LT. STEIN: Lieutenant Studdard.

LT. STUDDARD: Lieutenant Stein.

LT. STEIN: Long time no see.

LT. STUDDARD: Mm hm.

Pause.

LT. STEIN: Any ideas on this one?

LT. STUDDARD: Mm.

LT. STEIN: No?

LT. STUDDARD: Sure. Some.

LT. STEIN: I wasn't briefed.

LT. STUDDARD: This is the briefing.

LT. STEIN: I know. Just that there was no overview.

Pause.

In my orders.

LT. STUDDARD: Me neither.

Pause.

Feel better?

LT. STEIN: Yes, thank you Lieutenant.

LT. STUDDARD: Mm.

Pause.

LT. STEIN: I made a point of getting here early.

Pause.

Did you become a specialist?

LT. STUDDARD: Communications. Mostly data retrieval.

LT. STEIN: I went into explosives.

LT. STUDDARD: I know Lieutenant Stein.

LT. STEIN: Okay.

Pause.

How did you know?

LT. STUDDARD: You carry a high profile Lieutenant

LT. STEIN: Right.

LT. STUDDARD: Multiplied by your sex.

LT. STEIN: There's that.

LT. STUDDARD: Sore thumb.

LT. STEIN: Scarlet letter.

LT. STUDDARD: One of those.

LT. STEIN: Yeah.

Pause.

I assume you read about the trouble at Fort Bragg.

LT. STUDDARD: Hm.

LT. STEIN: Not *my* trouble. *The* trouble. I don't think of it as *my* trouble.

LT. STUDDARD: That thing with the *Times* was you?

LT. STEIN: I assumed that was common knowledge.

LT. STUDDARD: I don't think it is.

LT. STEIN: That's good to know.

LT. STUDDARD: Either way. I didn't draw any conclusions.

LT. STEIN: Neither did the disciplinary committee.

LT. STUDDARD: Looks like you came out alright.

FREUD enters.

LT. FREUD: Well well well. Lieutenant Stein.

LT. STEIN: Lieutenant.

LT. FREUD: Harpo.

LT. STUDDARD: Mm.

LT. FREUD: What's the good word? Are we collecting Intel? Hostage rescue? Hm? Silent insertion? I love silent insertion. So romantic.

LT. STEIN: There hasn't been a pre-briefing.

LT. FREUD: No, of course.

LT. STEIN: Of course?

LT. FREUD: I didn't receive one.

LT. STUDDARD: Of course.

LT. FREUD: What do you know Harpo?

LT. STUDDARD: Very little Lieutenant Freud.

LT. FREUD: Come on Harpo. How long have we been friends? Every time I see you it's like we're starting over.

LT. STUDDARD: Hm.

LT. FREUD: (*To STEIN.*) We go way back. And you: I know you.

LT. STEIN: We've never met Lieutenant.

LT. FREUD: You sure? I feel like I know you.

LT. STEIN: I don't think so.

LT. FREUD: Didn't you convince me to join the Marines?

LT. STEIN: We haven't met.

LT. FREUD: We haven't?

LT. STUDDARD: Okay Travis.

LT. FREUD: What is it? 'The Marines, historically, have been leaders in racial and gender integration. Our project is righteous, the playing field is level, and the time…is now.'

LT. STEIN: Why were you watching a minority recruitment tape?

LT. STUDDARD: What's this?

LT. STEIN: I filmed a recruitment tape four years ago.

LT. STUDDARD: For minorities?

LT. FREUD: I'm one-fifth Portuguese.

LT. STEIN: How old are you?

LT. FREUD: That tape really worked. Little thing in tight jungle fatigues –

LT. STEIN: That's lovely. Thank you. Nice to meet you.

LT. STUDDARD: That's enough.

LT. FREUD: – And I get to carry a gun? As opposed to college?

LT. STEIN: Classy.

LT. FREUD: That makes you my manifest destiny. If you know what I mean.

LT. STEIN: I know what you mean Lieutenant.

LT. FREUD: Do you?

LT. STEIN: Sure I do. It's the sad reality of a volunteer army. A bunch of incentive-dependant videogame junkies with permanent erections take the place of men with heart and soul. Your enlisted class resembles that which is skimmed from the surface of old milk.

LT. FREUD: Jeez Louise. Charmed I'm sure.

LT. STEIN: You are charming. Trot around the world in heavy vehicles lending your brutality to countries unversed in the Tarzan logic of the old guard. I'm so glad I participated in recruitment.

LT. STUDDARD: I think that's enough.

LT. FREUD: What? Did I beat your high score on 'Ms Pacman' at Fort Brag?

LT. STEIN: I don't do the smile and nod thing Freud.

LT. FREUD: Harpo, do you appreciate the significance of this pairing? She's the mother of my military career.

LT. STUDDARD: How old are you?

LT. FREUD: The horizon line of my heroic trajectory in this beloved Corp.

LT. STEIN: Don't let my tits be your substitute horizon Freud. That's what the desert is for.

LT. FREUD: What tits? Who said anything about tits?

LT. STUDDARD: Language. Watch your language.

LT. FREUD: No, my mistake. I should trust the bathroom walls for my inside information. Most soldiers doubt you're human. A cyborg. An immaculate conception.

LT. STEIN: I heard test tube baby.

LT. FREUD: Same fucking thing.

LT. STUDDARD: Language.

LT. FREUD: Oh sorry Harpo. I don't possess your stoicism. Teach me.

LT. STUDDARD: For the tapes.

LT. STEIN: What tapes?

LT. STUDDARD: (*Indicating the microphone above them.*) We're live.

LT. FREUD: Live to where?

LT. STUDDARD: Don't know. I wired at 0700.

LT. STEIN: You were here first?

LT. FREUD: Why are they taping us?

LT. STEIN: I'm not sure I'm comfortable with this.

LT. FREUD: Unless, maybe for an audio manual. Maybe this is a non-standard op.

LT. STEIN: No.

LT. FREUD: It stands to reason.

LT. STEIN: This is a briefing for a *mission*, correct?

LT. STUDDARD: Yes.

LT. FREUD: Who cares anyway? I've got nothing to hide.

LT. STUDDARD: Victory forgives dishonesty.

LT. STEIN: Well the Colonel isn't here and I'm not comfortable with surveillance.

LT. FREUD: You aren't comfortable?

Pause.

LT. STEIN: I'm not comfortable with anything supplemental and unnecessary.

LT. FREUD: The cover of the *New York Times* – that's no problem – but this.

LT. STUDDARD: Travis.

LT. FREUD: What, isn't it common knowledge? Your star-studded debut as an unnamed source?

LT. STEIN: You can't make me blush Lieutenant.

LT. FREUD: I'm surrounded by spies. At least Harpo gets paid to tattle.

LT. STUDDARD: I do data retrieval.

LT. STEIN: Behave yourself and you've got nothing to worry about.

LT. FREUD: Turn around is fair play.

LT. STEIN: If it degrades the quality of our performance: I'm not comfortable with it.

LT. FREUD: Anxiety is good for your performance.

LT. STEIN: My performance record doesn't need any improvement.

LT. FREUD: Performance without anxiety is like a day without sunshine.

LT. STEIN: (*To STUDDARD.*) Lieutenant, is this going to be a cowboy mission? I don't do cowboy missions.

LT. FREUD: That's my favorite kind of mission.

LT. STEIN: That's something I might have predicted.

LT. FREUD: The problem is: Are their enough healthy Indians?

LT. STEIN: Studdard?

LT. STUDDARD: I don't think so. I think this is low profile.

LT. STEIN: With microphones?

LT. FREUD: How ironic. The marine's shining star prefers the cover of night. A woman after my own heart.

LT. STEIN: I like standard, well-organized, government-sanctioned murders. I'm not a goddam cold-war spy.

LT. FREUD: Marines don't murder. They *shape* the enemy.

LT. STEIN: He's a starving artist.

LT. STUDDARD: This makes sense.

LT. STEIN: What?

LT. STUDDARD: (*Jerking his head toward LT. FREUD.*) Sniper.

LT. STEIN: (*To LT. FREUD.*) You're a sniper?

LT. FREUD: I prefer hopeless romantic.

LT. STUDDARD: This must be a minor target mission.

LT. STEIN: Single building or complex?

LT. STUDDARD: I don't know, that's your thing. I'm guessing three to five targets.

LT. FREUD: You know: There is a great deal of mythology surrounding my role, but precious little respect.

LT. STEIN: Did you receive equipment specs?

LT. STUDDARD: Hm.

Short pause.

LT. STEIN: And?

LT. STUDDARD: Four voice-activated open-channel mics. Four twelve-hour battery packs. A mess of jamming equipment and four PBBs.

LT. STEIN: What is that? Protective Body what?

LT. STUDDARD: Personal Black Box.

LT. FREUD: Oh I love those. You can compose your own breathless eulogy.

LT. STEIN: I didn't receive any equipment specs.

LT. FREUD: 'Tell my girlfriend she's pregnant.'

LT. STEIN: Lieutenant Freud?

LT. FREUD: Yeah?

LT. STEIN: Did you receive equipment specs?

LT. FREUD: I brought my gun. But I always bring my gun.

LT. STEIN: I don't do minor target missions and I don't do black ops.

LT. FREUD: What 'don't'? Meaning what?

LT. STEIN: I'm not qualified for para-military ops.

LT. FREUD: What are you qualified for?

LT. STEIN: I do pre-demo. Foundation corruption. Structural contamination. I've done some remote ambush detonation.

LT. STUDDARD: I thought you did the palace banquet in '94?

Pause.

LT. FREUD: *You* did the palace banquet?

LT. STEIN: I *planned* and *supervised* the palace banquet.

LT. STUDDARD: Did you design the instruments?

LT. STEIN: I built and designed the instruments but I was a half-mile away supervising detonation with a commando unit. I never entered the target site.

LT. FREUD: Did you carry?

LT. STEIN: I'm a marine lieutenant. I carry a fucking gun.

LT. STUDDARD: Language.

LT. FREUD: Listen to you. I'm jealous of the attention you give that microphone.

LT. STEIN: And how do you know about the palace banquet? That was a black-op.

LT. FREUD: Exactly.

LT. STEIN: My *only* black-op.

LT. STUDDARD: Makes sense.

LT. FREUD: Every new day in the uniform is a rash of favors and exemptions for you princess.

LT. STEIN: I doubt very much you'd trade places with me.

LT. FREUD: I would. If only to assume responsibility for that dirty deed. Truly brilliant.

LT. STUDDARD: I've seen the satellite photos from that.

LT. FREUD: Exploding soup bowls. Spoon shrapnel. Flammable tablecloth. And then she dropped the fucking roof on them.

LT. STUDDARD: I remember.

LT. FREUD: It was a whimsical attack. The first truly whimsical remote assassination.

LT. STUDDARD: What flavor soup?

LT. STEIN: I didn't cater the fucking –

Pause.

Crab.

LT. STUDDARD: How many?

LT. FREUD: It was twelve.

LT. STEIN: Thirteen. One target. Six sons. Six daughters.

LT. STUDDARD: They were collateral?

LT. STEIN: No, they were consistent obstructions.

LT. FREUD: See? Black-ops aren't so bad.

LT. STEIN: It's unsportsmanlike. It leaves a bad taste in my
mouth.

LT. FREUD: Nahhhhh. Blacks-ops are like blind dates. The
bigger the risk the brighter the fireworks.

LT. STUDDARD: Unless the target is unworthy.

LT. FREUD: True Harpo. If she's a dog you just close your
eyes and think of Hitler.

LT. STEIN: I'll thank you not to use generic feminine
pronouns Lieutenant Freud. We're co-ed today.

LT. FREUD: What if the target is a woman?

LT. STUDDARD: It won't be.

LT. FREUD: Okay. You know something we don't Harpo?

LT. STUDDARD: I can only imagine.

LT. STEIN: I believe the Colonel is late.

LT. FREUD: Every target has a feminine side – present
company excluded.

LT. STEIN: Watch yourself Lieutenant.

LT. FREUD: Now I should watch myself? Why don't you
get with my program Lieutenant? What are you, FTA?

LT. STEIN: I graduated top of my class Lieutenant. I have
no Failure To Adapt. I very much doubt recruit training
was more difficult for me than for you. You're the cocky,
undisciplined lout.

LT. STUDDARD: Hm.

LT. FREUD: Kiss my grits.

LT. STEIN: Let me make something very clear Lieutenant. I'm not sitting in this room as a party favor nor will I knowingly participate in the degradation of my rank. I'm perfectly willing to spar a bit but I won't tolerate anything that smells like disrespect.

LT. FREUD: Pardon me Lieutenant. I'll make a more genuine effort to conceal my odor.

LT. STEIN: That's all I ask Freud.

LT. FREUD: Thank you Lieutenant.

LT. STEIN: Thank *you* Lieutenant.

COL. JOHNS enters. All move to stand, almost sit, and then stand at attention.

COL. JOHNS: Okay. At ease Marines. Please take a seat. I'm glad to see you've chosen to arrive early. This briefing will last approximately thirteen minutes during which time you will be rewarded with all knowledge relevant to this mission. I also hope we can learn a bit about each other as we will be working together intimately over the next seventy-two hours.

Pause.

Everyone here? Lieutenant Studdard?

LT. STUDDARD: I wouldn't know sir.

COL. JOHNS: Of course. Sure. You're all here. To Begin: Imprecision. Folly. Sacrifice. (*LT. FREUD coughs.*) Question? No. Okay. Imprecision. Folly. Sacrifice. These are the contagions which are bound to infect any mission executed without proper planning, indoctrination, and passion. My experience tells me these pitfalls widen when a mission bears the extra burden of secrecy.

Unfortunately, without secrecy, there would be no clear path to victory, and there we are. Questions? Alright. You'll be assassinating 'Big 'Stach', hereby referred to from this moment until his timely demise as 'The Bearded Lady'. Questions?

Pause.

Any questions?

LT. STEIN: Sir, with all due respect, three Marine battalions and the third infantry spent three months trying to locate –

COL. JOHNS: 'The Bearded Lady.'

LT. STEIN: 'The Bearded Lady.' I'm certain the quality of intel could not be strong enough to deploy a small unit….

COL. JOHNS: The intel is waterproof.

LT. FREUD: Sir, Lieutenant Travis Freud, Fort Poke: Sir, though your proposition intrigues me I would like to pose a question.

COL. JOHNS: Go ahead Lieutenant.

LT. FREUD: It is my understanding that 'Big – '

COL. JOHNS: 'The Bearded Lady.'

LT. FREUD: 'The Bearded Lady' suffers from a range of psychological disorders exasperated by his decadent isolation and extreme wealth. Delusions, paranoia, impotence –

COL. JOHNS: Yes Lieutenant. What is your question?

Pause.

LT. FREUD: Well, I suppose it wasn't so much a question as a comment sir.

COL. JOHNS: Thank you for that Lieutenant. Lieutenant Studdard?

LT. STUDDARD: Fine sir. Only I'm unclear as to my role.

COL. JOHNS: 'Every marine a rifleman', Lieutenant.

LT. STUDDARD: I understand sir.

COL. JOHNS: Primarily you'll be responsible for recording and editing and hour-by-hour audio document detailing the mission. This will be used primarily as a training tool for black-op procedure and, in the event that this document is misinterpreted, or becomes the subject of misinterpretation, you will be expected to toilet this particular document. Alternately, if our actions are celebrated, you will prepare excerpts for distribution.

LT. STUDDARD: I doubt anything will have to be destroyed Colonel.

COL. JOHNS: Not sure I understand you there Lieutenant.

LT. STUDDARD: The least common response to my work is misinterpretation.

COL. JOHNS: Sure thing. Victory forgives dishonesty. Any further questions before we adjourn for the day?

LT. STEIN: Yes sir. How are we going to do it?

COL. JOHNS: Okay sure. Sure thing. We can do that now. I suppose. Sure. Mission plan: You have ten hours special equipment / recon training, a portion of which will require you to familiarize the team with your specialty. A sixteen-hour flight to the desert, and approximately twelve hours to complete your mission, eight of which will be occupied with undercover travel. Our intel is our primary advantage – that and a secure contact with a native rebel unit, which will provide access to the mansion.

LT. STEIN: The mansion?

COL. JOHNS: Yes. With any luck the target will be between silk sheets at the time of intrusion.

LT. STUDDARD: What about doubles?

COL. JOHNS: Decoy and double identification will be part of your recon training, though I've also authorized the elimination of any doubles or look-a-likes.

LT. FREUD: Sir, every man in the country is a look-a-like.

COL. JOHNS: Point taken Lieutenant. Point taken.

Pause.

This is in many ways a standard op. Lieutenant Freud will eliminate perimeter guards –

LT. FREUD: How many perimeter guards?

COL. JOHNS: – Lieutenant Studdard will disable enemy communication systems. Lieutenant Stein, you'll be blowing the door and rigging the place for a forensic wipeout. During this time Studdard and Freud will eliminate the target.

LT. STEIN: Who is functioning as unit commander?

COL. JOHNS: I will be your unit leader Lieutenant Stein, following this briefing I'll be entering special training alongside all of you. Any questions?

LT. FREUD: With all due respect Colonel, wouldn't your wisdom and considerable military experience be better utilized from a secure location?

COL. JOHNS: A secure location? Maybe a chair with rockers or wheels Lieutenant? I am fifty-one years old and I have very low cholesterol. Does that quiet your concern?

LT. FREUD: Sir –

COL. JOHNS: Let that quiet your concern.

LT. STEIN: Sir?

COL. JOHNS: Yes Lieutenant Stein?

LT. STEIN: Are we to expect any international or domestic backlash against a clandestine political assassination?

COL. JOHNS: I'm sure there will be some.

LT. STEIN: Exactly how big of a backlash, in your estimation?

COL. JOHNS: How big? Well, how long is a piece of string?

Pause.

LT. STEIN: Colonel, sarcasm isn't necessary.

COL. JOHNS: No really: How long is a piece of string?

Pause.

LT. STEIN: I simply asked for your estimation.

LT. FREUD: Nine inches. That's my guess.

COL. JOHN: Thank you Lieutenant Freud. Does that answer your question Lieutenant.?

LT. STEIN: Colonel do we have a choice?

COL. JOHNS: A choice Lieutenant?

LT. STEIN: Do we possess the option to decline this mission?

COL. JOHNS: I consider your commitment to this mission a choice Lieutenant. And I believe you've made the right choice.

LT. STEIN: That is not a choice I've made.

LT. STUDDARD: Emma...

COL. JOHNS: I think you should tread lightly Lieutenant.

LT. STEIN: Permission to speak freely Colonel?

COL. JOHNS: I'll grant you permission to articulate your confusion about the definition of 'choice'.

LT. STEIN: I'm not confused as to the definition sir. I'm unclear as to the conditions which shape that choice.

Pause.

COL. JOHNS: Speak freely Lieutenant. What would make you happy?

LT. STEIN: Sir: Happy will it be if our choice should be directed by a judicious estimate of our true interests, unperplexed and unbiased by considerations not connected with the public good.

Pause.

LT. FREUD: Colonel, this might be a good time to let you know that Lieutenant Stein does not speak for me. Lieutenant Stein's career is inoculated against the consequences of dissent. Mine, like many, is nourished by obedience.

COL. JOHNS: Or something resembling obedience?

LT. FREUD: Whatever you like, Colonel.

COL. JOHNS: And how do you feel Lieutenant Freud?

LT. FREUD: Feel?

COL. JOHNS: Yes Lieutenant.

LT. FREUD: Permission to speak freely?

COL. JOHNS: Yes yes, go ahead.

LT. FREUD: Sir, our true interests are for you to know and me to fire at the target. I'd rather not share a pillow with the public good.

COL. JOHNS: Studdard? Would you like to make a formal statement regarding your involvement in this mission?

LT. STUDDARD: I stand not with the advocates of disunion.

COL. JOHNS: Who is your advocate?

LT. STUDDARD: The dead will speak for me sir. I remain neutral.

COL. JOHNS: A historian never confesses his bias.

LT. STUDDARD: A historian has no bias.

COL. JOHNS: Good boy. As to your happiness Lieutenant Stein: Happiness is a thing more ardently to be wished than seriously to be expected. Regarding your choice: Our passions will color this thankless affair, lending glory to an otherwise tawdry event. We will be the bigger men, architects of liberty. We will sacrifice ourselves, but first and foremost, we will sacrifice the lives of our enemies, and school them in the manners and etiquette of death. We will seduce their bodies and steal their breath, bury them with heads pointing toward Mecca, and collect memories of their forgotten cause. (*To STUDDARD.*) That'll be your job. As their race is the chosen body of our righteous intervention, we will honor their unfortunate wishes and make every effort to preserve the dignity of their ravished corpses. Each corpse will index our cause, and document the unfolding destiny of this magnificent empire.

Pause.

And if there is nothing else I'd like to direct you to the mess hall for hot dogs and salad. Dismissed. Lieutenant Stein, my office please.

Pause.

COL. JOHNS exits.

31

LT. FREUD: You'll thank me later.

LT. STEIN: Yeah, with a brick.

LT. FREUD: Promises promises.

LT. STUDDARD: Do you know where the mess hall is Emma?

LT. STEIN: I'll find it.

Transition.

LT. FREUD: You're eating salad.

LT. STUDDARD: I don't eat hot dogs.

LT. FREUD: Why not?

LT. STUDDARD: It's garbage civilian food.

LT. FREUD: Don't be a hard-ass Harpo.

LT. STUDDARD: It gives you the runs.

LT. FREUD: 'Garbage Civilian Food'. You're such a leatherneck.

LT. STUDDARD: Lieutenant Freud, you're so unconventional.

LT. FREUD: Okay. You wanna race? First one to eat five hotdogs.

LT. STUDDARD: No thanks.

LT. FREUD: No buns. Just the dogs. Make it ten. But you can't drink anything in between.

LT. STUDDARD: I'd be afraid to win.

LT. FREUD: You're afraid to win?

LT. STUDDARD: Sure.

LT. FREUD: A marine should never be afraid to win.

LT. STUDDARD: We're talking about hot dogs, right?

LT. FREUD: Okay, fifteen hot dogs. No mustard.

LT. STUDDARD: You have a very volatile personality.

LT. FREUD: You don't fool me Studdard. Race me with hot dogs. You know you want to.

LT. STUDDARD: Hm.

LT. FREUD: I eat unconscious desires for breakfast.

LT. STUDDARD: Uh huh.

LT. FREUD: What's your excuse Studdard? Did someone touch you a long time ago?

LT. STUDDARD: If at first you don't succeed, redefine success.

LT. FREUD: Okay Yoda. I call you coward.

LT. STUDDARD: Then call me.

LT. FREUD: Coward. What kind of marine would refuse a plate of fine pork hot dogs? This is life reconstituted into a delicious and compact form. This hot dog will fit in your throat and slide out your ass. It is the distillation of some swine's hopes and dreams, the reordered flesh of a once noisy creature. Someone took the raw material of life and transformed it into something meaningful, and beautiful and delicious. And it is your responsibility to consume this hot dog and transform it into energy; energy which will assist you in the seduction and evaporation of our enemies. There is no such thing as a vegetarian killer Harpo. This is also true of artists like myself. An artist breeds, bleeds, and consumes the best part of this world. Race me with hot dogs. I promise: You'll shit a sculpture too radiant for words, sign the canvas and have a glass of wine.

Pause.

33

LT. STUDDARD: Do you want your apple pie?

LT. FREUD: Yes.

LT. STUDDARD: Okay. First one to finish fifteen gets the other's dessert: One…

Transition.

COL. JOHNS: Alright Lieutenant. Maybe I don't look like a pacifist to you. Maybe I'm just one more gray crew cut in a long line of faceless father figures. Maybe I'm some pitiless jarhead with no sense of direction, so I took a job that lets me carry a compass. Maybe I'm just a babysitter to you, and you're just waiting for mom and dad to come home. But I think you misjudge me Lieutenant. I think I can make you comfortable here. I can help you out of that dress and into something more comfortable. I want to negotiate a treaty with that body Lieutenant, and do business with your mind.

LT. STEIN: Sir, I don't waste time dodging exploitation. You want me in front of cameras with medals on my chest? I'll be there. My mind, and my ability, speaks for itself. Anything else you want me to say: I'll say it.

COL. JOHNS: You are everything we need and everything we don't. A PR dream wrapped in a logistical nightmare. A pretty face – evidence of the glory of American democracy, equality, and integration – or someone's daughter in a body bag, crippling the resolve of our loyal hawks.

LT. STEIN: What do you want from me Colonel?

COL. JOHNS: Apart from your co-operation I don't want anything from you Lieutenant. You aren't here to be the celebrity grunt. I wanted a lonely-hearts club. Bachelors and childless women. Bearers of the scarlet letter of loneliness. We want to be sure our passions don't dilute our focus.

LT. STEIN: Is that all Colonel?

COL. JOHNS: I'll let you be the soldier you want to be Lieutenant. Good with bombs. Anonymous. Just give me some loyalty. Keep this mission off the cover of the *New York Times.*

LT. STEIN: You shouldn't worry about my loyalty to the cause Colonel Success is my feminism, unrestricted by any crisis of conscious.

COL. JOHNS: I thought punctuality was your feminism?

LT. STEIN: (*Looks up at microphone.*) I was here on time wasn't I?

Transition.

LT. FREUD: Hey Stein.

LT. STEIN: Lieutenant.

LT. FREUD: Go ahead and tell her Harpo.

LT. STEIN: Tell me what?

LT. FREUD: I've robbed Lieutenant. Studdard of his fragile masculinity.

LT. STEIN: Super.

LT. FREUD: Seriously, when does life get hard? I'm ready to jump out and scare life. Recent victories have stiffened by resolve.

LT. STEIN: Did you see cheeseburgers up there, or just hamburgers?

LT. FREUD: If the marines don't kill me I'll have to journey to the center of the earth and ingest its creamy vanilla filling.

LT. STEIN: I don't think we're in good hands with the Colonel.

LT. STUDDARD: What makes you say that?

LT. STEIN: I think he's a feminist.

LT. STUDDARD: I thought he was a nihilist?

LT. FREUD: Feminist, nihilist: Same fucking thing.

LT. STEIN: Pass the carrots.

LT. STUDDARD: What did he want to talk about?

LT. STEIN: He's one of those.

LT. STUDDARD: Which?

LT. STEIN: Advocates of Sensitive Leadership.

LT. FREUD: Was he gentle?

LT. STEIN: I think he wants to be my friend.

LT. FREUD: God forbid.

LT. STUDDARD: He's from the new school.

LT. FREUD: A little old for the new school isn't he?

LT. STEIN: Probably just a Failure To Adapt. All the older brass have daddy issues.

LT. FREUD: Or political aspirations.

LT. STEIN: Same thing.

LT. FREUD: She gets it.

LT. STUDDARD: What did he actually say?

LT. STEIN: He's an acid casualty. Probably never read the Constitution. He thinks war is his personal masturbation fantasy.

LT. FREUD: Whatever floats your boat.

LT. STEIN: Whatever floats his boat.

LT. STUDDARD: He seemed fine when I talked to him this morning.

Pause.

LT. STEIN: You talked to him this morning?

LT. FREUD: You can talk?

LT. STEIN: Before the briefing?

LT. STUDDARD: I had a pre-briefing this morning.

LT. STEIN: You said you didn't.

LT. STUDDARD: I said there was no overview in my orders.

LT. FREUD: Come on Stein, don't play dumb. Harpo is internal affairs. You can't trust a word he says. He baby-sits that tape.

LT. STEIN: Fine. You had a pre-briefing. You could of told us we were working for John Juan up there.

LT. FREUD: Don.

LT. STEIN: What?

LT. FREUD: Don Juan. Not John Juan. I'm one-fifth Portuguese.

LT. STUDDARD: I didn't see any reason to be concerned.

LT. STEIN: He's creepy.

LT. FREUD: It's a good thing we cut danger out of the war thing, otherwise I'd be worried.

LT. STEIN: I'm not worried. I'm concerned.

LT. FREUD: Let go and let God.

LT. STUDDARD: God has nothing to do with it.

LT. FREUD: How about arm-wrestling? Would you like to arm-wrestle? Recover some dignity?

LT. STUDDARD: You didn't capture my dignity.

LT. FREUD: I didn't?

LT. STUDDARD: You didn't.

LT. FREUD: Well what is this in my stomach? It doesn't feel like a belly full of hotdogs. It kicks and turns like a frightened dignity covered in soft fur and searching wildly for it's father. Not to worry dad: Your dignity will remain imprisoned in my guts until it crawls from my busy birth canal twelve hours from now—at which point I will gently suggest that you reabsorb this brown orphan. Orally.

LT. STEIN: Jesus, my appetite is not the enemy.

LT. STUDDARD: If my dignity is in your guts why don't I just go in and get it.

LT. FREUD: That sounds mildly erotic.

LT. STUDDARD: It was meant to sound violent.

LT. FREUD: It didn't.

LT. STEIN: (*Looking* up.) These tapes aren't being archived, by the way. They're being reviewed daily.

LT. STUDDARD: That's standard protocol.

LT. STEIN: Standard for what?

LT. FREUD: You wanna arm-wrestle Stein? I can't get a rematch from 'He-who-hath-surrendered-his-dignity'.

LT. STUDDARD: I want to clarify that he ate twelve hot dogs faster than me. That's what happened.

LT. FREUD: That's the problem with the official record Harpo, it has no odor.

LT. STUDDARD: I'm losing my patience with you.

LT. FREUD: Your patience and your dignity? This just isn't your day.

LT. STEIN: Stop it please. I give up, okay? You are both hard as nails with nerves of steel. I'm very impressed. Now no more pissing contests. I'm trying to eat.

LT. FREUD: That's a good idea. We'll have a pissing contest. Wait, I'm the only one with a dick. How about a little arm-wrestling?

LT. STEIN: You don't fool me Freud.

LT. FREUD: I don't?

LT. STEIN: I know you just want to hold hands.

LT. FREUD laughs.

LT. STUDDARD: This is going to be a long week.

LT. FREUD: You're quite the little filibuster. Would you like to have nine of babies?

LT. STEIN: That task would likely require half the energy of tolerating a single conversation with you.

LT. FREUD: Well, that's my new hobby: Watching steam come out of your ears.

LT. STUDDARD: I have to go get ready.

LT. STEIN: Evolve or die. That's all I've got to say.

LT. FREUD: Is that all you have to say?

LT. STEIN: That's it.

LT. FREUD: Well, happy birthday to me.

Transition.

LT. STUDDARD: Satellite microphones.

COL. JOHNS: Oh?

LT. STUDDARD: I developed a new type of satellite microphone. Better range and clarity.

COL. JOHNS: Well, why don't I just bring the satellite microphones and leave you behind?

LT. STUDDARD: I don't know. I assume because of my interpretation skills.

COL. JOHNS: You speak Arabic?

LT. STUDDARD: No.

Pause.

COL. JOHNS: Go ahead Lieutenant Studdard.

LT. STUDDARD: There are ten major encryption protocols used in the region, which correspond to the executive. launch codes outlined in 1988. We will be utilizing two simultaneous frequencies which will compliment each other and, in all likelihood, fill in for each other in case of regional or weather-related disturbance.

COL. JOHNS: Can you just give us the long-and-short of it?

LT. STUDDARD: Not really Colonel.

COL. JOHNS: Just give us the essence, the spirit of it.

LT. STUDDARD: Sir, in the event of my incapacitation the 'spirit' of our communication frequency isn't going to rise up and take charge.

COL. JOHNS: Well, there are no atheists in the foxhole.

LT. FREUD: What's a foxhole?

LT. STUDDARD: With all due respect sir, atheists make the best historians.

COL. JOHNS: No, deconstructionists make the best historians.

LT. STUDDARD: Sir, I'm not sure that even makes sense.

LT. FREUD: Colonel, can we go?

LT. STEIN: What 'we'? I'm not going anywhere with you.

COL. JOHN: Is this really you Lieutenant? You couldn't possibly be this boring.

Pause.

LT. STUDDARD: Hm.

COL. JOHNS: Make us *feel* why your role is important. Make us *care* that you're alive for God's sake. I like our *target* more than I like you.

LT. STUDDARD: Sir, I thought I was supposed to…

COL. JOHNS: Make us *feel* encryption protocols.

LT. STUDDARD: Sir, there is no feeling in what I do. I establish the lines of communication. I record. I translate. I archive. I'm either calling it in or writing it down. I'm not tongue-kissing anyone.

COL. JOHNS: Can you believe this Lieutenant Stein?

LT. STEIN: Sure, I've known Studdard a long time.

COL. JOHNS: Freud?

LT. FREUD: I'm beside myself.

COL. JOHNS: What is history Studdard? Is it a terribly good excuse to bump heads? Is it the best argument against hope?

LT. STEIN: It is a terribly good excuse to bump…

COL. JOHNS: It's a bedtime story.

Pause.

LT. STUDDARD: Should I continue or…

COL. JOHNS: It's the most dangerous narcotic on the market. You'd think advances in high-speed media technology would help people kick the habit of history, but we've got stubborn, dusty addicts like you producing and distributing hot shots all over the place.

LT. STUDDARD: Sir, every conflict has a context.

COL. JOHNS: What's so special or so comforting about a back-story?

LT. STUDDARD: Colonel I'm proud to be part of the most sensitive fact-checking organization in the world.

LT. FREUD: He's very sensitive.

COL. JOHNS: Well are you a stenographer or a soldier?

LT. STEIN: Sir, can I say something?

COL. JOHNS: Go ahead Lieutenant.

LT. STEIN: I think Lieutenant Studdard is trying to say that those who don't know history are doomed…

COL. JOHNS: Let me be doomed. What's the big deal with being 'doomed to repeat'? I'm alive aren't I? I woke up this morning. I wouldn't mind repeating that

LT. STEIN: I just don't think its necessary…

COL. JOHNS: As long as I'm alive please, let me be doomed to repeat. I'd rather be alive and ignorant than dead and 'sensitive to the facts'. We've got a nation of teenage poets cultivating a rich crop of sensitivity. Where do I get my warriors?

LT. STUDDARD: Sir, someone has to…

COL. JOHNS: We'll need a government program to breed tough litters of clueless enforcers, raised in video arcades, isolated from all this poisonous 'history'.

LT. STUDDARD: Colonel I'm…

COL. JOHNS: I think this mission will be good for you Lieutenant… Help you use your left-brain.

LT. STUDDARD: You mean my right brain?

COL. JOHNS: One of those.

Pause.

LT. STUDDARD: Permission to speak freely Colonel?

COL. JOHNS: Only if you're planning to account for this little fetish for evidence. And only if you're planning to explain how this kinky little ritual wins wars.

LT. STUDDARD: Sir, I believe all rhetorical questions are accusations.

COL. JOHNS: Is that it?

LT. STUDDARD: Sir, any absence of passion is a by-product of my pitiless career. I'm a baby-sitter. I take care of the words when they lose their bodies. That's my job. I don't need a heart. I've got reels of incriminating evidence. I handle spools of careless conversation. I preside over a kingdom of sound bites and transcripts.

Pause.

Would you like to know why I'm quiet? Is that your question? Why I refrain from all your chatter? I know where loose talk goes to die. Loose talk is slow to decompose. I know the generous afterlife of gossip. I know how easy it is to make a memory. There is a reason that peace and quiet are partners. This is why a soldier prefers deafness. Because the blind are condemned to a life of eavesdropping. Have any of you spent a significant amount of time eavesdropping? You'll beg for deafness.

Pause.

I've got enough passion and chatter collecting dust on my shelf, Sir.

Pause.

COL. JOHNS: Okay. That was good. Freud, can you familiarize us with your role later this afternoon?

LT. FREUD: Yeah, that'll be fun.

Transition.

LT. STEIN: That's him.

COL. JOHNS: Freud?

LT. FREUD: I'm saying that's the double.

COL. JOHNS: Studdard?

LT. STUDDARD: The double.

Pause.

COL. JOHNS: That's him.

LT. FREUD: What is wrong with me?

LT. STEIN: Travis, did you get a copy of the identification brochure?

LT. FREUD: Harpo didn't get it right either.

LT. STEIN: Am I the only one who has actually taken the time to study this goddam CENTCOM twelve-step identification brochure?

LT. FREUD: Well I still don't think that's him.

COL. JOHNS: Well, Lieutenant Freud, you just misidentified the primary target. We don't want any missed opportunities.

LT. FREUD: Hey, I guessed it was the double. That doesn't mean I'm not taking the shot.

LT. STEIN: Then what's the point Travis?

LT. FREUD: There is no point. I'm clipping anything with a mustache.

COL. JOHNS: Lieutenant Freud. Let's take this seriously.

LT. FREUD: Oh, I'm serious. You said we're taking out the doubles. Why do we need to spend seven hours learning how to do mole-to-pupil distance ratios?

COL. JOHNS: Why Lieutenant Studdard?

LT. STUDDARD: We have to know where and when we hit 'The Bearded Lady', otherwise we won't know when we're done.

COL. JOHNS: I thought you'd be good at this Lieutenant Freud.

LT. STEIN: I'm not wasting my primary instrument on a body-double Freud.

LT. FREUD: Well, you're scoring ninety per cent so don't worry about it.

COL. JOHNS: Fine. Lieutenant Studdard, what was the source of your miscalculation?

LT. STUDDARD: Well sir, I'd like to point out that I've been going third, so my first instincts are being influenced by Stein and Freud's guesses.

LT. FREUD: Okay, that's my excuse too.

LT. STEIN: What are you, a collie dog? Don't use your instincts Harpo, employ the goddam rational method of analysis outlined in the CENTCOM brochure.

LT. STUDDARD: Emma, I was up all night…

COL. JOHNS: Lieutenant Stein, how did you know this was 'The Bearded Lady'?

LT. STEIN: It was a combination of the mild cauliflower around the ear and the redundant tissue in the cheeks.

LT. STUDDARD: The jowls?

LT. STEIN: That's more than a set of jowls, that's redundant tissue.

COL. JOHNS: I wouldn't rely on that if I were you.

LT. STEIN: I'm scoring ninety per cent.

COL. JOHNS: Okay, put down that goddam brochure. It isn't working.

LT. STUDDARD: Colonel I just didn't have any time to review the brochure in detail…

COL. JOHNS: Forget the brochure. It didn't work for Freud.

LT. STUDDARD: With all due respect sir…

LT. FREUD: Don't say it Harpo.

COL. JOHNS: Try this one.

Pause.

LT. STEIN: That's the double.

LT. STUDDARD: Okay. The double. I'm guessing double.

COL. JOHNS: Look at the eyes Freud. Do you notice a certain quality?

LT. FREUD: Brown.

COL. JOHNS: No. I mean, yes, brown. But do you notice a vaguely seductive quality?

LT. STEIN: What? Is that the target?

COL. JOHNS: Would you like to change your guess?

LT. STEIN: No. That's the double.

COL. JOHNS: Lieutenant Freud?

LT. FREUD: I don't know. The double?

COL. JOHNS: That's the target.

LT. STEIN: That can't be him. The mole placement isn't right.

COL. JOHNS: She's wearing make-up. We can't pin down the location of that beauty mark with any certainty. Look at the eyes.

LT. STEIN: Are you positive Colonel?

COL. JOHNS: Look at the eyes Stein. That's our target. Do you see it? Freud? What do you see?

LT. FREUD: A vaguely seductive quality?

COL. JOHNS: Bedroom eyes.

LT. STEIN: Bedroom eyes?

COL. JOHNS: She's like dove.

LT. FREUD: Yeah. With a mustache.

LT. STEIN: I'm not sure 'bedroom eyes' will register through infrared goggles.

LT. FREUD: I don't know how we're supposed to see anything in these crappy photos anyway. Who took these?

LT. STUDDARD: I took these.

COL. JOHNS: Are you picking up what I'm putting down here Studdard?

LT. STUDDARD: Sir, I'm not even sure what bedroom eyes are.

COL. JOHNS: Bedroom eyes. You know. Like Rudolph Valentino. Or Raul Julia.

Pause.

LT. STEIN: No, it's the frown lines. The frown lines are a dead giveaway.

COL. JOHNS: The eyes don't lie.

LT. STUDDARD: Maybe if I redesign Freud's scope?

LT. FREUD: Sir, why don't you slip between the sheets. That way we can be certain we've eliminated the Arab with the kindest eyes.

COL. JOHNS: I'm disappointed Lieutenant.

LT. FREUD: Colonel I honestly can't tell them apart.

LT. STUDDARD: What if I redesign your scope?

LT. FREUD: I don't use a scope. I use opera glasses.

Transition.

LT. STUDDARD: 'Dear American Heroes, Hello. I am ten. My dad says it's okay to hate the war but we shouldn't hate the soldiers because they are poor high school. dropouts from rural areas. Then again, the U.S. Army does possess the largest class of black executives of any major private or government body.' Is that true?

LT. STEIN: I don't know. Is he in private school?

LT. STUDDARD: Read yours.

LT. STEIN: 'Dear Army Man' – Great I get the ten-year-old sexist.

LT. STUDDARD: All ten-year-olds are sexist.

LT. FREUD: Don't these little crumb snatchers know the goddam difference between the Army and the Marines?

LT. STUDDARD: What's the difference Travis?

LT. STEIN: 'I am nine years old. Could you beat up my dad in a fight? My teacher says 'Big 'Stache' is like Hitler. This comparison must refer to Hitler's legacy of ethnic and religious genocide, rather than his nationalist grab for global power which would correspond more accurately to the contemporary American policy of…' Is this supposed to boost my morale?

LT. FREUD: Little know-it-all. I'm glad I skipped fourth grade.

LT. STEIN: Blah blah blah 'nation-building' blah blah 'Christian war machine' blah blah love Tommy, Burlington Vermont.

LT. FREUD: 'Christian war machine'?

LT. STUDDARD: Kids say the darndest things.

LT. STEIN: What'd you get?

LT. FREUD: 'Dear Hero, My mom says America is the most immoral, totalitarian force in modern history. But if that is true, how come we have the biggest kitchens in the world?'

LT. STUDDARD: How does he know?

LT. FREUD: She.

LT. STUDDARD: How does she know we have the biggest kitchens in the world?

LT. FREUD: Blah blah 'charred remains of Iraqi babies' yadda yadda 'peace be with you' love, some Asian kid. Why does everyone love babies so much? Every asshole you ever met was a baby!

LT. STUDDARD: I don't want to kill babies.

LT. FREUD: Wars should be fought by babies. They're the most cold-blooded little assholes AND they don't care if they live or die.

LT. STEIN: Stop trying to be shocking. Babies are the reservoirs of human potential.

LT. FREUD: Everyone loves babies all of a sudden! What are you pro-life?

COL. JOHNS: Why are you talking about babies?

LT. STUDDARD: Freud thinks wars should be fought by babies.

COL. JOHNS: Why?

LT. STUDDARD: Because they are cold-blooded and fearless.

COL. JOHNS: Forget it. You need empathy to fight a war. Babies have no empathy.

LT. FREUD: I don't have empathy.

LT. STEIN: Even I don't have empathy.

COL. JOHNS: Trust me, you've got empathy.

LT. FREUD: Not Studdard though. He definitely doesn't have it.

LT. STUDDARD: I couldn't even define it.

LT. FREUD: Well sure! I can't *define* it.

LT. STEIN: You can't define empathy?

LT. FREUD: I'm a sniper, not a playwright. Can *you* define it?

LT. STEIN: Sure: It's a noun meaning 'the ability to understand and share the feelings of another'.

LT. FREUD: Use it in a sentence.

LT. STEIN: Oh shut the fuck up.

COL. JOHNS: 'The sniper empathized with his target, reflecting woefully on the brutal dance of death just prior to pulling the trigger.'

LT. STEIN: Wouldn't the presence of empathy stop him from pulling the trigger?

COL. JOHNS: On the contrary. That's my point.

Pause.

No.

LT. FREUD: I don't want empathy.

LT. STUDDARD: I guess I don't know what I'm missing.

LT. STEIN: You're not missing much. Muscle-memory beats empathy every time.

LT. FREUD: It's like rock-paper-scissors.

COL. JOHNS: But empathy beats intelligence.

LT. STEIN: Muscle memory, intelligence… / Same fuckin' thing.

LT. FREUD: Same fuckin' thing. Great minds.

LT. STUDDARD: Colonel, should we reseal these letters and forward them to the Navy?

COL. JOHNS: Very funny Harpo, give me the goddam letters.

LT. STEIN: That was good.

LT. FREUD: Funniest thing he's ever said.

LT. STEIN: Fuckin' kids.

LT. FREUD: Who needs 'em.

Transition.

COL. JOHNS: Okay, this the nice part.

LT. STEIN: I hate this.

COL. JOHNS: We've got to leave something nice underneath the tree.

LT. FREUD: If only they had trees.

LT. STUDDARD: Where are we dropping these?

COL. JOHNS: These are the most current standard-issue care packages, which are to be distributed proportional to the number of targets planned or improvised.

LT. STUDDARD: We're playing tooth fairy.

COL. JOHNS: Problem Studdard?

LT. STUDDARD: Not at all.

LT. STEIN: Put them under the pillow.

LT. FREUD: I ain't no fairy.

LT. STEIN: I saw that coming.

COL. JOHNS: We're cutting back on the food bank stuff. Nothing keeps in that heat.

LT. FREUD: I thought Lieutenant Stein was in charge of the 'care packages'.

LT. STEIN: Cluster packages. Thank you.

COL. JOHNS: You'll be the good cop, she'll be the bad cop.

LT. FREUD: I can't be the good cop. I'm playing cupid.

LT. STUDDARD: I'll drop the packages.

COL. JOHNS: Thank you Lieutenant.

LT. STEIN: Is that how we're wrapping them?

COL. JOHNS: The paper is recyclable.

LT. FREUD: You can't trust them to recycle.

LT. STUDDARD: What's inside? Do I have to hold them upright?

LT. FREUD: 'Is that how we're wrapping them?'

LT. STEIN: It's bright orange.

COL. JOHNS: Each package contains: One protein bar. Honey-peanut I think. One miniature white flag. A calculator. And three condoms.

LT. STEIN: They should get candy.

LT. FREUD: No, they need our protein.

LT. STUDDARD: Condoms?

COL. JOHNS: And then we've got these cartoons. Which are instructional.

LT. STUDDARD: What do they need condoms for?

LT. STEIN: Ooo, let me see the cartoons.

LT. FREUD: It's like: 'Immigrate to the U.S., and you might need these.'

LT. STUDDARD: Hm.

LT. FREUD: 'Provided you shave your dirty beard.'

LT. STEIN: Look at this, this is total propaganda.

LT. STUDDARD: Lets not use the word 'propaganda'. (*Looks at microphone.*)

COL. JOHNS: Watch it Stein.

LT. STEIN: Okay, what is 'The Bearded Lady' doing in this picture?

LT. STUDDARD: I think that picture speaks for itself.

LT. FREUD: It's a harmless allegory.

COL. JOHNS: Nothing would be crueler than the truth. Consider our enemies coddled by this propaganda.

LT. STEIN: Do you think because you drew an arrow from 'The Bearded Lady' to a pile of money that his people will rise against him?

LT. FREUD: More importantly, will they know that's a stack of ones?

COL. JOHNS: A strong narrative arch is essential to any military victory. You should know that.

LT. STEIN: This narrative arch has poor character development.

COL. JOHNS: Let me worry about the sentence structure. Studdard will pick the descriptive nouns. Freud will provide colorful adjectives. You worry about the exclamation point at the end.

LT. FREUD: Fuckin' Charlie Rose over here.

LT. STEIN: Why are we dropping this shit? Why are we operating 'under cover of night'. If this operation is such an international blockbuster why are fiddling around with care packages and agit-prop and fucking maps and manifestos and mission statements? What the fuck kind of ethical stand needs to be figured out at a conference table?

LT. FREUD: Ethical what now?

COL. JOHNS: Do you need to get some water Lieutenant Stein?

LT. STEIN: Is it just me? Studdard? Shouldn't the wisdom and logic of any mission be self-evident? I don't want to waste a perfectly good instrument on a half-baked grudge killing that is in constant need of cosmetic tinkering.

LT. STUDDARD: Alright Emma, don't quote Ben Franklin just because you want the nation to admire you fireworks.

LT. STEIN: It has nothing to do with vanity.

LT. STUDDARD: Not every soldier in this unit desires recognition above all things.

LT. FREUD: You're not exactly famous for keeping your finger in the dyke.

COL. JOHNS: You're too self-involved Lieutenant Stein. You need to think about someone else for a change.

LT. STEIN: I seem to be the only one attending to the big picture.

COL. JOHNS: You want a big picture? They either love us or they love to hate us. Either way we're spreading love.

LT. STEIN: It's chaos. Not affection.

COL. JOHNS: You think 'The Bearded Lady' wants to be left alone? More importantly, do you think 'The Bearded Lady' wants to come out on top? We could call him up – Studdard has his phone number – and say 'Hey Bearded Lady, be my leader. Put my wife in a big sock and take away my magazines.' Do you think he'd be happy? In no way. In no way would he be happy. Everyone loves an underdog.

LT. FREUD: If we didn't kick that guy's ass no one would know he existed. He'd never get laid.

LT. STEIN: Aren't you the one that wants to do the laying Cupid?

LT. FREUD: I'm killing two birds with one stone.

COL. JOHNS: That's why they call it the 'little death' Lieutenant, because it's a fine line between orgasm and eternity.

LT. STUDDARD: I thought it was because your heart skipped a beat.

LT. STEIN: That's sneezing.

LT. STUDDARD: What are we talking about?

LT. FREUD: Listen to me Emma, his cock-sucking religion says when I kiss him goodnight he gets to nail sixty-nine virgins or whatever. We're doing him a favor.

LT. STEIN: It says he's 'met' by sixty-nine virgins, it doesn't say anything about 'nailing them'.

LT. FREUD: Well what are they going to do, wash his back?

COL. JOHNS: 'Met' by virgins. 'Met' is biblical code for 'screwed'.

LT. STEIN: Biblical code? He doesn't read the bible!

LT. FREUD: What are you? A prisoner of conscious?

COL. JOHNS: 'Koran' is Arabic code for 'Bible'. Right Studdard?

LT. STUDDARD: No.

COL. JOHNS: Look at me? Tell me I don't respect the dignity of our target? I'm dressed up like her goddam ancient Mesopotamian landscape tapestry of indigenous plant life.

LT. FREUD: His underwear is desert-camo.

LT. STEIN: You have no idea do you? I can't be a part of a failed mission. I can't ride shotgun on an aborted black-op. Do you have any idea happens when missions involving women fail? Women lose their pensions.

COL. JOHNS: What do you suggest Lieutenant Stein?

LT. STEIN: I think we should tighten this up a little. At the very least we should double our personnel.

LT. FREUD: Fucking 'personnel'. This isn't Office Depot.

LT. STUDDARD: She means manpower.

LT. FREUD: Whatever.

LT. STEIN: We shouldn't rely on native informants.

COL. JOHNS: We're not planning a wedding.

LT. STEIN: Yes we are. That's exactly what we are Planning. That's what the Palace Banquet was – the entire reason I'm stuck in this ridiculous black-op – the Palace Banquet was a well-catered, tasteful affair with a carefully considered guest-list, hand-printed invitations and expensive cake. This mission is a sloppy tongue kiss.

LT. FREUD: Well you can put a woman in uniform but you can't…

COL. JOHNS: This isn't our first date with the target Stein. I think we've earned the right to slip her the tongue.

LT. STEIN: That's just it Colonel It isn't our first attempt on 'Big 'Stache'. It's the fifth. What will make this attempt work?

COL. JOHNS: Your considerable talent.

LT. STEIN: Well I don't want a suite of flatterers. I want a finished project.

LT. FREUD: You mean a corpse?

LT. STEIN: We don't want the same things Freud. Trust me. If you were running the show we'd still be in Vietnam.

LT. FREUD: Darn tootin'.

COL. JOHNS: You've got a lot to learn Lieutenant Stein. About the Order of Things.

LT. STEIN: What order? What order?

COL. JOHNS: You've got a lot to learn from those bombs of yours Lieutenant Bombs don't love the plan. Bombs love the enemy.

LT. STEIN: Then you don't need me.

COL. JOHNS: You can see a bomb adapt to the conditions of life in half a second.

LT. STEIN: I quit.

COL. JOHNS: Say that again Lieutenant.

LT. STEIN: I quit.

COL. JOHNS: I'll see you in my office Lieutenant Stein. Now.

Transition.

COL. JOHNS: You think I need you more than you need me?

LT. STEIN: I don't think you need me sir. I think you're stuck with me.

COL. JOHNS: Maybe Lieutenant.

LT. STEIN: It's okay to be against women in the military sir. I am.

COL. JOHNS: I don't object to you Lieutenant, I object to a world too weak to see you in a body bag. I hate the delicate sensibilities of househusbands and working moms who love integration but hate death.

LT. STEIN: I hate death, sir.

COL. JOHNS: Let's change that, shall we?

LT. STEIN: I'm in the habit of hating death sir, and old habits die hard.

COL. JOHNS: I think your mother taught you something and you forgot to forget it.

LT. STEIN: What does my mother have to do with this?

COL. JOHNS: What the child knows is parental detritus. Garbage thought. The leftovers of a mind destroyed by age.

LT. STEIN: I thought you believed in wisdom sir.

COL. JOHNS: I believe in the radiance of my own enlightenment. Your parents? I don't trust them.

LT. STEIN: Tell me sir, what did I forget to forget?

COL. JOHNS: There is no such thing as progress Lieutenant. Only passion, and the lack thereof.

Pause.

LT. STEIN: A marine would never imagine this mission sir. Only a politician would be so undisciplined as to pray for instability.

COL. JOHNS: That isn't your call Lieutenant. You don't have to love the boss, you just have to love thy enemy, and learn to fuck her gently until she ceases to breath.

Pause.

LT. STEIN: My marine code is governed by morality sir, and a belief in social change.

COL. JOHNS: Are you a pacifist Lieutenant? I am.

LT. STEIN: Negative sir. Even Darwin knew explosions were good.

Pause.

COL. JOHNS: You bomb specialists are all the same. It's all about the Big Bang. If evolution held any water we would have evolved our way out of death! That appears to be the giant pink skid-mark on your doctrine of progress that no one wants to talk about. Wait, let me guess, 'It's coming!' Is that it? We'll 'get there'? 'Sit tight.' 'All things in good time.' It *is* evolution after all; 'all things…' including immortality, 'in good time'. You're like Jesus freaks with your voodoo evolution, I swear to Doug. You believe in progress? Why? Because the landscape is dotted with a greater number of incontinent grannies clutching the handrail so they don't blow away? Fucking longevity is humanity's botched nose-job. Look at me. I'm a disgusting mess of expired worm food. I'd take myself off the shelf if Jesus would let me.

LT. STEIN: Take me off the mission, Colonel.

COL. JOHNS: You don't want me to take you off the mission.

LT. STEIN: I do Colonel.

COL. JOHNS: I want you to be my ally Lieutenant. I want to hold on to our lion-hearted women even as the feminine leaves our body politic. Let it evaporate and travel with the clouds. Let it rain on darker people in dryer nations.

LT. STEIN: But I don't think I need your assistance. My success begs respect. I don't have to say a word.

COL. JOHNS: Let other nations give birth to our children, Lieutenant. They're good at it.

LT. STEIN: Do I look like I have children?

COL. JOHNS: You don't want off this mission. You've been detonating phone books and false alarms at Fort Ticonderoga for the past nine months. No one will touch you. You're damaged goods. You want perfection? I'm the only one giving you a chance to fail.

LT. STEIN: I did what responsible soldiers do. I went public. I never asked for any special favors.

COL. JOHNS: Nobody asks for special favors but when they are offered it is not customary to refuse.

LT. STEIN: Customary no. Honorable, yes.

COL. JOHNS: You don't want special treatment. You don't want special assignments. You want to do the work, even when it's dirty. You will defer to the superior wisdom of those in command, perform for the cameras when the cameras need a story. You have no secondary allegiances to your sex or your sisterhood. You hate death and love progress. That's your story?

LT. STEIN: There are worse indignities than explanation.

COL. JOHNS: I know about your past. Your loose lips. Your talent with bombs. That's the best alibi in a military overflowing with toothless volunteers. Honest to God talent kicks dirt all over the footprints of a cum-stained career…

LT. STEIN: I'm a lot of things. But I'm not helpless.

COL. JOHNS: How can I trust a damsel that seems to be in love with her own distress?

LT. STEIN: It seems the more honest I am the less people trust me.

COL. JOHNS: I don't like honesty. I like loyalty.

LT. STEIN: I am loyal to the principle of a public good.

COL. JOHNS: Who are you trying to impress? It's just me here. You want me to shut off the tapes?

LT. STEIN: No sir. I refuse to exist off the record.

Pause.

COL. JOHNS: Okay Lieutenant. Have it your way.

LT. STEIN: You can sign the dismissal papers in the morning.

COL. JOHNS: No Lieutenant. I'm putting you in charge.

LT. STEIN: Sir?

COL. JOHNS: Out with the old. In with the new.

LT. STEIN: Colonel I can't…

COL. JOHNS: I'll let you be the soldier you want to be. I'll follow your lead.

LT. STEIN: Sir. You can't.

COL. JOHNS: I made a promise. I intend to keep it. You're in charge of all operational maneuvers.

LT. STEIN: You think I'm incapable.

COL. JOHNS: Not at all. I'm embracing your remedy to the sickness Lieutenant, don't be ungrateful.

LT. STEIN: Why sir?

COL. JOHNS: Just make sure you keep Freud in line. Understood?

LT. STEIN: Yes Colonel. Thank you Colonel.

Transition.

COL. JOHNS: What do you think about Travis and Emma?

LT. STUDDARD: I don't think about them.

COL. JOHNS: Take a minute then.

LT. STUDDARD: What's to think? I entered the marines so I wouldn't have to think.

COL. JOHNS: Is that it? Has discipline eroded your instinct for gossip? Are you a cyborg? Have we collapsed your capacity for prejudice?

LT. STUDDARD: I have opinions. I just don't remember them.

COL. JOHNS: I need you to be my eyes and ears on this mission.

LT. STUDDARD: Why not refer to the instant replay? (*Indicating the microphone.*)

COL. JOHNS: Look. I've got to misplace my trust somewhere, why can't it be with you?

LT. STUDDARD: Why not consult Lieutenant Freud? He has a gift for interpretation.

COL. JOHNS: Is that what you want? You want me to talk to Freud? Aren't you worried what he'll say about you?

LT. STUDDARD: I don't worry much.

COL. JOHNS: That's good.

Pause.

That's good. I'm going to tell you something. Just you. I'm going to share something with you. You and I will be doing things. differently. Travis and Emma, we'll let them continue as before.

LT. STUDDARD: What do you mean?

COL. JOHNS: One must harness their passions, but never let those passions get the best of them. I never doubt the beauty of a target. We need her symmetry in this cock-eyed world of indecision. The brass, they haven't always understood the broader implications of our target's pleasant odor in this world. I'm telling we are going to explore this relationship without necessarily consummating it.

LT. STUDDARD: Sir.

COL. JOHNS: We're not going to kill the target.

Pause.

LT. STUDDARD: So the mission is canceled?

COL. JOHNS: I see no reason to do that.

LT. STUDDARD: Then what are we going to do?

COL. JOHNS: I don't know, flirt a little. Deliver some flowers. It'll be our little secret.

LT. STUDDARD: Why are you telling me this?

COL. JOHNS: I wouldn't tell you Lieutenant, unless I needed some help keeping this thing from getting out of hand.

LT. STUDDARD: What about Stein and Freud?

COL. JOHNS: They will learn to love again. I assume you'll be content to wallow in indifference?

LT. STUDDARD: Not indifference. Neutrality.

COL. JOHNS: Same fuckin' thing.

LT. STUDDARD: Sir, Freud is one thing, Stein is another. Lieutenant Stein is a very capable and driven soldier. Her enthusiasm for the mission is unmatched.

COL. JOHNS: That's why I'm putting her in charge. Her enthusiasm has led to cardinal sin. Stein has fallen in love the plan. We won't bother to redirect her affections. We'll let her be the public face of our failure. You and I can enjoy the benefits. Does that make sense Lieutenant?

Pause.

LT. STUDDARD: Is this an order?

COL. JOHNS: Yes, it is an order.

LT. STUDDARD: Then it doesn't have to make sense.

Transition.

LT. STEIN: I submit to you, this design, in full confidence that your delicate touch, which has often marked prior affairs, will allow a smooth execution; sensitivity to all due weight and effect is necessary.

LT. FREUD: I'm becoming hugely unoptimistic about this mission.

LT. STEIN: I've still got you on trigger duty Travis. Don't be sad. I am sanctioning a boycott of the flaccid and joyless scene into which advocates of peace would conduct you.

LT. STUDDARD: Are we calling this a change of plans?

LT. FREUD: Is it just me, or has this promotion gone to your head?

LT. STEIN: It'll be a masterpiece. As to our anonymity, it's a shame. Why do we have to do it as a black-op Harpo?

LT. STUDDARD: We won't know until it's over.

LT. STEIN: Why is this a black-op? Are they trying to save money?

LT. STUDDARD: Save face maybe.

LT. STEIN: From what?

LT. STUDDARD: Maybe congress won't play ball. Maybe the allies feel carsick. It might be more cost effect than a public invasion.

LT. STEIN: Is that everything you know?

LT. STUDDARD: Maybe it's a test mission. Testing the waters. Maybe it's meant to register public opinion.

LT. STEIN: Okay, so we're the foot they lower into the bath.

LT. FREUD: More like the thermometer they shove up the target's ass.

LT. STEIN: What did this guy actually do?

LT. STUDDARD: Colonel Johns?

LT. STEIN: The target.

LT. FREUD: Who cares?

LT. STUDDARD: He's your average neighborhood philistine. Lots of big ugly magical-realist portraits and boring television.

LT. FREUD: Is that the official record?

LT. STUDDARD: I think that's the real reason I'm on this mission. I bugged his house in '94.

LT. STEIN: Well is he actually dangerous?

LT. STUDDARD: He's a bad guy. Why not kill him?

LT. FREUD: Hear hear.

LT. STEIN: It isn't perfect, but I've worked with less. If we make it look like an accident, or a domestic dispute we can completely eliminate any fallout or backlash. We'll need to toilet the care packages and any traceable ballistics or explosive components.

LT. FREUD: Poor tools require better skills.

LT. STEIN: What's our worst-case scenario?

LT. STUDDARD: It'll probably stir up the region. Lawlessness. Financial instability.

LT. FREUD: Sounds like freedom to me.

LT. STEIN: I'll thank you not to use the f-word around me Lieutenant. This isn't 'Little House on the Prairie'.

LT. FREUD: This is fast becoming the most clinical, unromantic affair I've ever wasted four shots on.

LT. STEIN: You like to have fun don't you Freud? Do you think freedom is fun?

LT. FREUD: No, I hate it. I want to go to prison.

LT. STEIN: You'd shrivel up and die if there weren't any rules to break.

LT. FREUD: You've got something on him don't you? I know this isn't a merit-based promotion. You've got dirty photos of him nursing a bird back to health.

LT. STEIN: Stop playing dumb Travis.

LT. FREUD: I don't just play dumb, I write and direct.

LT. STEIN: You don't fool me.

LT. FREUD: Right, because you're exceptional. You go anywhere you don't belong so you can be special and miserable and persecuted and collect undeserved favors and papal indulgences.

LT. STEIN: I'm making a point.

LT. FREUD: About what? Freedom? About how freedom sucks? We aren't talking about the freedom in the abstract you fucking twat. We're talking about hungry little countries where you die *because* you break the rules.

LT. STEIN: Who got you so excited about fighting oppression? You're a fucking MARINE, you signed up for a job where your boss can force you to do push-ups. You love oppression.

LT. FREUD: Yeah, but I *signed up* for it.

LT. STEIN: So you invade dirt farms in unpronounceable corners of the world so that the citizenry might one day elect to discipline itself? Why not skip the middleman?

LT. FREUD: And the starving class will never know the Judeo-Christian ecstasy of a diet regime. And the limbless will miss out on decades of aerobics. And the impoverished radicals will never know the joy of wasting a privilege. And I know this is a word game where you get me to 'admit' I like buttfucking?

LT. STEIN: Don't you think marines are better than civilians?

LT. FREUD: Yes.

LT. STEIN: Why?

LT. FREUD: Why?

LT. STEIN: Yes.

LT. FREUD: Because we're more disciplined.

LT. STEIN: My point. We love the way they beat it out of us. And we're trapped. By a compulsion to share.

LT. FREUD: It isn't the same.

LT. STEIN: You've never thought about what you do. You probably joined the marines so people would stop asking your opinion.

LT. FREUD: So what are you? A hooker with a heart of gold? Are you a cyborg struggling to let the human side take over.

LT. STEIN: There are two methods of removing our malignant opposition: the one, by extinguishing the liberty which is essential to its existence; the other, by giving to all peoples the same opinion, the same passion, and the same interests. I'm ambitious. I want both. I want rules and regulation. I want patterns of behavior. I want lexicons and manuals. There is no emotion Freud. Only a plan. A set of predictions. The conditions. The results. No evil. Just our hypothesis. The test. The results.

LT. FREUD: Well you're old school. I don't like your game. It doesn't make me feel good. I don't care if everything lines up. That's what you don't realize. I'm new school. You want to be part of an occupying army, with a benevolent philosophy. Correcting the chaos and teaching them how to fucking recycle. Well I don't want to recycle. I don't want to keep our planet green. I want to live on a fragile planet. I want to fuck on the verge of extinction.

Transition.

COL. JOHNS: Finally we make the transition from ground to sky. American culture comes off like wet corduroys on a hot day doesn't it kids?

LT. STEIN: Is that a good thing?

LT. FREUD: I can't wait to go native.

LT. STEIN: How long until the drop?

COL. JOHNS: It's surprisingly hard on the ankles.

LT. FREUD: Your ankles.

COL. JOHNS: I'm young at heart.

LT. STEIN: Studdard, we're going to go over the itinerary.

LT. FREUD: Worst thing about drops is trees. I don't see any trees.

LT. STEIN: Studdard!

LT. STUDDARD: Emma, I told you I have a goddam headache.

LT. STEIN: We aren't going to 'play this by ear'. Lets review the procedure.

COL. JOHNS: I think everyone knows their role Lieutenant Stein.

LT. STEIN: I want to minimize the need for improvisation.

LT. STUDDARD: We're going to rendezvous with land support at 2300 hours.

LT. STEIN: Where?

LT. STUDDARD: Half mile from the drop zone.

COL. JOHNS: Everything looks so calm and democratic from this height. Disappointment is in the details, I'll tell you. That's what my father said.

LT. STUDDARD: We'll be riding in the back of civilian truck to grid point E12 which is approximately two miles from the hot spot.

LT. STEIN: Are we approaching from the front or the back?

LT. FREUD: I'm telling you right now: We aren't using that driver.

LT. STUDDARD: The driver is going to get us through two checkpoints.

LT. FREUD: Forget it. I'm clipping that fool. I'll drive.

LT. STEIN: Colonel?

COL. JOHNS: Look at it! It could be Tijuana from up here.

LT. FREUD: It could be Tijuana from down there.

LT. STEIN: You're not clipping anyone unless I say so Lieutenant.

LT. FREUD: We'll drive around the goddam checkpoints. It's the fucking desert.

LT. STUDDARD: Travis, that'll cost us two hours.

LT. FREUD: I'm superstitious.

COL. JOHNS: Hey: I haven't washed this uniform in six years.

LT. STEIN: I'm warning you Travis, we won't be sidetracked by any improvisational flourish or superstitious hokey-pokey.

COL. JOHNS: You mean hanky-panky.

LT. FREUD: You'll regret the loss of my trust Emma. That was your life raft in this mission.

LT. STUDDARD: Can it. Seriously. Fucking can it.

COL. JOHNS: Can it!

LT. STUDDARD: Colonel.

COL. JOHNS: You can it! Everyone can it! Everyone be silent. Enjoy the delicate sounds of destiny.

LT. FREUD: I might be a prisoner of conscious, but there is still enough room in here (*Indicating his head.*) for bloodlust and a little common sense.

LT. STEIN: It isn't common sense if you're the only one who thinks so.

COL. JOHNS: Can it! Fucking CAN IT! Now can't you two see that you're in love with each other? We can't have that. What about 'The Bearded Lady'? What is she supposed to do? What about the lonely target? Who will keep her warm at night with you two wasting all this heat on each other?

LT. STEIN: I was just going to go over that. Our man will deliver us to the hot spot. Lieutenant Freud will not be clipping the driver.

LT. FREUD: Can I shave his mustache?

LT. STEIN: The Colonel and Lieutenant Studdard will be positioned outside the perimeter wall of the compound. When Studdard has disabled the security system and cut the phones, myself and Lieutenant Freud will enter mansion and do the deed. Nothing too difficult.

COL. JOHNS: If there are any problems we will simply abort the mission.

LT. STEIN: We aren't aborting anything.

LT. STUDDARD: We're two minutes from the drop.

LT. STEIN: Get ready Freud. This is your chance to clean up that spotty combat record?

LT. FREUD: Those spots are blood.

LT. STEIN: Your body should be manipulated by authority, rather than imbued with animal spirits.

LT. FREUD: Well who is delivering the killing blow on this mission? Who is assuming the ultimate responsibility? When will I be awarded with some trust? Let me explain something: As long as I'm the trigger man on this mission I'll expect oodles and oodles of room to breath for every petty superstition, gut feeling, sixth sense –

LT. STEIN: How much room do you need?

LT. FREUD: – Every facial tic, muscle spasm, and bathroom break will be lovingly accommodated by you, and you, and…

LT. STEIN: How much room do you need?

LT. FREUD: Unless you want to pull the trigger? You want that responsibility?

LT. STEIN: I would cherish that responsibility.

LT. FREUD: Good, it's yours!

LT. STEIN: But it isn't my role. My responsibility is to the big picture.

COL. JOHNS: That's modern romance.

LT. FREUD: Take it, you're the triggerman now!

LT. STEIN: Are you insane? Are you suffering from…

LT. FREUD: I'm suffering. Certainly suffering; from a case of bad faith and menstrual cramps. I'm suffering by proximity.

LT. STUDDARD: Grow up Travis.

LT. FREUD: AHHHH! Give me your job Harpo, instead of push-ups I'll cultivate moral superiority.

LT. STUDDARD: I was born with that.

LT. FREUD: You're cruising for a bruising.

LT. STEIN: I hope you put that parachute on upside down.

COL. JOHNS: Leave your memories behind. We need to travel light.

LT. STEIN: Should I leave my brain behind?

LT. FREUD: You'll definitely have more fun.

COL. JOHNS: Just bring your heart. That's the muscle that pulls the trigger.

Transition.

LT. STEIN: We're in position Colonel.

LT. STUDDARD: Colonel, they are in position.

COL. JOHNS: Hold position.

LT. STUDDARD: Hold position Stein.

LT. STEIN: We're holding.

COL. JOHNS: We haven't been detected?

LT. STUDDARD: Negative sir. I'm hearing every land and mobile line. There is no activity.

LT. FREUD: You know, if this were a proper sniper mission I'd have a nest.

LT. STUDDARD: Keep this line clear Lieutenant Freud.

LT. FREUD: Christ.

LT. STUDDARD: Colonel. They are in position to advance.

COL. JOHNS: Do they still have visual contact?

LT. STUDDARD: Lieutenant Stein, I'm going to send a visual signal, it should register on your northwest horizon line. Come back.

LT. STEIN: I'm waiting Lieutenant.

LT. STUDDARD: That's ABC, 123, over.

LT. FREUD: What are we waiting for?

LT. STEIN: Studdard is sending a visual signal.

LT. STUDDARD: Lieutenant?

LT. STEIN: Affirmative. I'm reading ABC123 in the my northwest corner.

LT. STUDDARD: Affirmative Colonel. I'm put them about two miles from our location.

LT. FREUD: Are we advancing?

COL. JOHNS: What time is it?

LT. STUDDARD: Sir, it is 4:35am local time.

COL. JOHNS: I should have let Freud drive around those checkpoints. We should be ten miles lost by now.

LT. STUDDARD: They are positioned perfectly Colonel.

COL. JOHNS: Do you know why Lieutenant Freud is on this mission?

LT. STEIN: Something is wrong.

LT. FREUD: Is he responding?

COL. JOHNS: 'Cause he's a goddam screw-up. He is ranked last among marine snipers. How do you like that?

LT. STUDDARD: What about Emma?

COL. JOHNS: Lieutenant Stein's career was over nine months ago. Can we stall them any longer?

LT. STUDDARD: Colonel, we're actually ahead of schedule.

LT. STUDDARD: Ask them if they can see the mansion?

LT. STUDDARD: Lieutenant Stein, can you see the mansion?

LT. STEIN: Affirmative Lieutenant. We could see the mansion from our previous position.

LT. STUDDARD: Colonel they can still see the mansion.

COL. JOHNS: No obstructions?

LT. FREUD: Are we going or what? I can see three potential targets from here.

LT. STUDDARD: Lieutenant is your view still unobstructed?

LT. FREUD: Tell me what he's saying. Harpo, come back.

LT. STEIN: Harpo, what the fuck is going on?

LT. FREUD: Are they giving an order? What's the order?

LT. STUDDARD: Lieutenant, is your view unobstructed? Come back.

LT. STEIN: He is asking if our view is still unobstructed?

LT. FREUD: No, there's a redwood forest in the way. Permission to burn it down?

LT. STUDDARD: Come back.

LT. STEIN: Lieutenant, there are no obstructions. Permission to advance?

LT. STUDDARD: Their view is unobstructed sir.

COL. JOHNS: Alright, is Freud in position to eliminate the perimeter guards?

LT. STUDDARD: Lieutenant Freud. Come back.

LT. FREUD: What is it Harpo?

LT. STUDDARD: Can you execute movement two?

LT. FREUD: Affirmative, I just need to use two bursts.

LT. STUDDARD: He says he needs two bursts.

COL. JOHNS: Two bursts? Why?

LT. STUDDARD: Lieutenant Freud, hold. Movement two should be a single burst, six seconds.

LT. STEIN: What is it?

LT. FREUD: I need to use two bursts.

LT. STEIN: Okay.

LT. FREUD: Movement two is one burst.

LT. STEIN: I can authorize two bursts.

LT. STUDDARD: Lieutenant Freud, movement two should be a single burst…

COL. JOHNS: This is it. We can pull them out.

LT. FREUD: Harpo, I've been sitting here for ten minutes. A single burst will put down guards one and two but most likely put our third man on the run. We can't risk a fast-moving target at this distance. He could duck behind that retaining wall and trigger an alarm.

LT. STUDDARD: He says a single burst will put man three on the run.

COL. JOHNS: Why would two bursts fix that problem?

LT. STEIN: Studdard, we need to move NOW. I can authorize two bursts.

LT. STUDDARD: Lieutenant Freud, why would two burst fix that problem?

LT. FREUD: Fuck this. I'm taking out the perimeter guards.

LT. STEIN: Just one second Travis…

LT. FREUD: Harpo, I'm taking my shots now.

LT. STUDDARD: You hold on Freud.

LT. STEIN: Just let me authorize the change in procedure.

LT. FREUD: Cover your ears.

LT. STEIN: Harpo, Harpo I'm authorizing two bursts.

LT. STUDDARD: Shit, he's taking the shot.

COL. JOHNS: Christ. Put her on my line.

LT. STUDDARD: Emma, I'm transferring you directly to Colonel…

Gunshot.

LT. STEIN: Shit Travis shit shit…

COL. JOHNS: Emma what the fuck are you…

Gunshot.

LT. FREUD: Man three rounding the corner.

COL. JOHNS: Hold fire Lieutenant. Now.

LT. STEIN: Colonel the movement is being executed.

LT. FREUD: Wait. Wait. Wait.

LT. STEIN: Take him out Freud.

COL. JOHNS: Lieutenant Stein, this isn't the plan.

LT. STEIN: Travis take the shot now he's about to –

Gunshot.

COL. JOHNS: Lieutenant Stein, what is going on?

LT. FREUD: Can you authorize all my maneuvers from now on?

LT. STEIN: Colonel with all due respect we are completing this mission.

COL. JOHNS: What happened to the plan Lieutenant?

LT. STEIN: Colonel, we can't allow our passions to dilute our focus.

LT. FREUD: You see that? Fucking gross.

COL. JOHNS: Take me off this line.

LT. STUDDARD: Emma, you're back on line with me.

COL. JOHNS: Tell them to hold position.

LT. STUDDARD: Hold position Emma.

LT. STEIN: Holding.

COL. JOHNS: It wasn't supposed to get this far. Oh Jesus. How did we get so close. This isn't where we want to be. FUCK FUCK FUCK FUCK.

LT. STUDDARD: Colonel, movement three puts them inside the mansion.

LT. FREUD: Do you feel that Emma? Those guys just became three of my best friends.

LT. STEIN: Can you get us inside the mansion?

LT. FREUD: Can you feel how much sense the world is making all of sudden?

LT. STUDDARD: It's Freud Colonel.

LT. STEIN: We are going to finish what we started. We are going to execute this plan.

COL. JOHNS: I guess that's love for you. Goddamit.

LT. STEIN: Harpo, we need to execute movement three right now.

LT. FREUD: Listen to you.

LT. STEIN: Shut the fuck up Travis.

LT. FREUD: Begging for permission to exist.

LT. STEIN: Harpo, we need to advance right now.

COL. JOHNS: Terribly good excuse to bump heads.

LT. FREUD: I feel sorry for you.

LT. STUDDARD: Colonel they aren't going to hold position.

COL. JOHNS: An index of this world's persistent delusion.

LT. STUDDARD: Colonel?

COL. JOHNS: Thank god we've still got Lieutenant Freud.

LT. STEIN: Harpo, we are executing movement three right now.

LT. STUDDARD: Negative Emma. Wait for our signal. Negative negative. Wait for confirmation.

LT. STEIN: You cover me Freud.

Transition.

LT. FREUD: Fuck this I'm going upstairs.

LT. STEIN: We don't have time Travis. I need to rig the instrument.

LT. FREUD: We need visual confirmation.

LT. STEIN: Travis YOU NEED TO STAY. The bomb will take care of everything.

LT. FREUD: You don't know how to have any fun.

LT. STUDDARD: Colonel she's going to set the instrument.

LT. FREUD: Are you as turned on as I am right now?

COL. JOHNS: Ten centuries won't teach us that love is to be avoided at all costs.

LT. STUDDARD: Colonel that bomb will level the entire building.

LT. STEIN: Harpo, I'm ready to set the instrument.

Pause.

LT. STUDDARD: Colonel she's in position. She's waiting for the order.

COL. JOHNS: FUCK FUCK. What happens if she sets that bomb?

LT. STUDDARD: Colonel 'Big 'Stache' is in the building. If she sets the bomb the target will be eliminated.

LT. STEIN: This is how it works Travis. This is how you accomplish something.

COL. JOHNS: I can't let her set that bomb Harpo.

LT. STUDDARD: What's the order Colonel?

LT. STEIN: I'm waiting for your order Colonel.

COL. JOHNS: I can't let her finish this mission Harpo. We need the target more than we need her.

LT. STUDDARD: Colonel.

COL. JOHNS: It isn't pretty, Harpo. You understand. Don't you? No more targets, no more history.

LT. STUDDARD: I understand.

COL. JOHNS: It didn't have to be this way. She's a good soldier. It's nothing personal.

LT. STUDDARD: It's nothing personal.

COL. JOHNS: She's good at what she does.

LT. STEIN: Harpo, I'm ready to set the bomb. I'm waiting for your order.

COL. JOHNS: Use Freud.

LT. STUDDARD: Should we try to pull them out?

COL. JOHNS: She won't pull out Harpo. Trust me. Use Freud. Use Freud.

Pause.

LT. STUDDARD: Lieutenant Freud.

LT. FREUD: What is it Harpo?

Pause.

LT. STUDDARD: There has been a change of plans.

LT. FREUD: Fuck your plans.

LT. STEIN: Quiet Freud.

LT. STUDDARD: Are you reading me Lieutenant Freud?

LT. STEIN: For a sniper you're not very precise.

LT. FREUD: I just fire at the shades of gray.

LT. STUDDARD: Travis, the target has changed.

Pause.

We're going to leave Emma there.

Pause.

That's the new plan.

Pause.

Lieutenant Freud, we don't want Emma to finish that bomb.

Pause.

LT. FREUD: What is this?

COL. JOHNS: She's the only target he's going to get.

LT. STUDDARD: Lieutenant, she is the only target you're going to get.

Pause.

Lieutenant, if you disobey this order it will be the last one you receive.

LT. STEIN: Progress is the only thing worth believing in Travis. This is what a good job looks like.

LT. FREUD: What does it look like Emma.

LT. STEIN: Like this. Like a perfect little bomb.

LT. FREUD: I don't know. I like to see the whites of her eyes.

He points the gun at her head.

LT. STEIN: Of course. You're a hopeless romantic.

LT. FREUD: I can't afford to be picky.

LT. STEIN: No. You're passionate.

LT. FREUD: Lieutenant Stein, do you want to have nine of my babies?

LT. STEIN: Quiet now Travis. 'The Bearded Lady' might hear you.

LT. FREUD: How about just one?

LT. STEIN: God, I love bombs.

Transition to a field recording.

LT. STUDDARD: Lieutenant Freud? Lieutenant Freud?

LT. FREUD: It's done Harpo.

COL. JOHNS: Let's get him out of there.

LT. FREUD: Am I leaving her here?

COL. JOHNS: Leave her.

LT. STUDDARD: Leave her there Lieutenant.

LT. FREUD: What about 'Big 'Stache'?

COL. JOHNS: You've had your fun Lieutenant. Come back.

LT. FREUD: What about the official record?

LT. STUDDARD: I've seen worse.

LT. FREUD: Should I pin a medal on her? Or are we waiting until the body comes home?

COL. JOHNS: Turn off the tape Harpo.

LT. FREUD: Lucky bitch.

LT. STUDDARD: Language.

LT. FREUD: You've seen worse.

COL. JOHNS: Turn off the tape Harpo.

Pause.

Turn off the goddam tape, n –

The End.